The Mystery
of
Stone Circles

Paul Mason

Heinemann Library
Chicago, Illinois

© 2002 Reed Educational & Professional Publishing
Published by Heinemann Library,
an imprint of Reed Educational & Professional Publishing,
Chicago, Illinois

Customer Service 888-454-2279

Visit our website at www.heinemannlibrary.com

Designed by AMR
Illustrations by Art Construction
Origination by Ambassador Litho Ltd.
Printed in China

06 05 04 03
10 9 8 7 6 5 4 3

Library of Congress Cataloging-in-Publication Data
Mason, Paul, 1967-
  The mystery of stone circles / Paul Mason.
     p. cm. -- (Can science solve?)
Includes bibliographical references and index.
Summary: Examines the phenomenon of stone circles and the various theories that exist to explain them.
  ISBN 1-58810-667-5 (lib.bdg.)   ISBN 1-58810-930-5 (pbk. bdg.)
  1. Stone circles--Juvenile literature. 2. Megalithic monuments--Juvenile literature. [1. Stone circles. 2. Megalithic monuments.] I. Title. II. Series.
  GN790 .M385 2002
  930.1'4--dc21
                            2001004537

Acknowledgments
The author and publishers are grateful to the following for permission to reproduce copyright material:
Science Photo Library, pp. 5, 12, 13, 15, 17, 24; Fortean Picture Library, pp. 7, 8, 10, 25, 27, 29; Rob Pilgrim, p. 11; Mary Evans Picture Library, pp. 14, 22; Fay Godwin/Collections, p. 16; Imagebank, p. 18; The British Museum, p. 19.

Cover photograph reproduced with permission of Robert Harding Picture Library.

Every effort has been made to contact copyright holders of any material reproduced in this book. Any omissions will be rectified in subsequent printings if notice is given to the publisher.

Some words are shown in bold, **like this.** You can find out what they mean by looking in the glossary.

Contents

It Is a Mysterious World

For tens of thousands of years, humans have found their surroundings strange and mysterious. Why does the sun sometimes disappear from the sky, blanked out by the moon? What causes the nights to get longer and the weather to get colder in winter? Why is the sky lit up by strange forked lightning during terrible storms? Science has found the answers to these questions.

This map shows the stone circles in Great Britain.

Other puzzles come from the past. One of the greatest mysteries surrounds the ancient stone circles that are scattered around France, England, Scotland, and Ireland. Many theories have been developed about these circles—about when they were built and what they were used for. But it was only after World War II that scientists began to study the stone circles more seriously, trying to discover the answers to some of these questions.

They have learned a lot of things, but they have also raised more questions. Some circles are simple—a few large stones arranged in a circle. Others are complicated and must have taken many generations to build. A few circles feature giant stones. Ancient people had only simple tools. How did they lift the stones, which weighed many tons, without modern machinery?

The secret language of the stones

barrow ancient grave mound

cairn mound of stones used as a marker of some kind

dolmen ancient tomb with a large, flat stone laid on top of upright ones

henge circular earth bank, often found around the outer edge of a stone circle

menhir single **standing stone**

Most of the circles have stood for thousands of years, and for most of that time, they have been a mystery to people who have seen them. At first, people simply wondered how they had been built, and why. But as we have discovered more about the stone circles, their mysteries have deepened.

The circle builders seem to have used mathematical techniques that scientists thought had not been discovered until long after the circles were built. Some circles were built from giant stones that came from hundreds of miles away. No one could figure out how they had been moved. Circles hundreds of miles apart were laid out using the same unit of measurement. Most mysterious of all, some of these ancient sites seemed to **align** with one another over huge distances.

With so many puzzles to solve, scientists had a real challenge

Stonehenge

High on the open landscape of Salisbury Plain in England stands the most famous, most studied, and most mysterious stone circle of all: Stonehenge. Many people first see Stonehenge from a distance, as they drive toward it. Seen this way, the stones appear quite small. But up close, their giant size becomes clear. The largest of them stands 18 feet (6.7 meters) high, and another 6.5 feet (2.4 meters) of the stone is buried below ground. If you were to stand on top of the stone, you could easily see into the second story windows of a house.

The Avenue

The way into Stonehenge is along a path known as the Avenue. It goes between two slopes of land called banks. At the entrance is a large red-stained stone lying on its side. People once thought the color was from human **sacrifices.** For that reason, it is called the Slaughter Stone. Scientists have now figured out that the color comes from rainwater reacting with the iron in the stone over thousands of years, not blood.

Stonehenge consists of several circles, each inside another. At the outside edge of the site are the Aubrey Holes, which were named after John Aubrey, who discovered them in the 1600s. The burned bones of human beings were found in the bottom of some of these 56 holes.

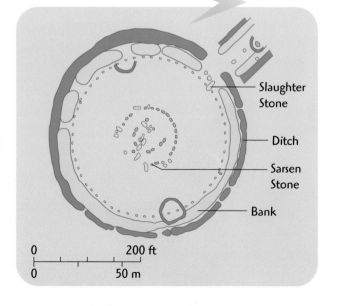

This is the layout of Stonehenge as seen from above.

Slaughter Stone

Ditch

Sarsen Stone

Bank

0   200 ft

0   50 m

The sarsen stones

The most dramatic part of Stonehenge is the central circle of giant **sarsen** stones. Some have now fallen or have been pushed over. Originally, they were arranged as a giant circle of upright stones, topped with another set of huge sarsens called **lintel** stones. Each group of three stones arranged in this way is called a **trilithon.** Some of the trilithons are still standing. It is hard to imagine how they could possibly have been erected without the help of some sort of crane.

This is part of the ancient circle at Stonehenge. For centuries, people were puzzled by how these giant stones had been moved into position.

Another mystery of Stonehenge is how the stones got there. Some of them come from a site in Wales more than 186 miles (300 kilometers) away. How could the people who built Stonehenge have moved the stones such a huge distance?

Strange Stonehenge

One of the earliest mentions of Stonehenge was made by the historian, Geoffrey of Monmouth. In 1135, he described several theories about how Stonehenge had been built. Some people claimed it had been brought to Ireland from Africa by a tribe of giants, then flown across the sea by the wizard Merlin. Other people said that the Devil stole the stones from an Irish woman, and then the stones were put on Salisbury Plain by Merlin for Ambrosius Aurelianus, the King of the Britons.

Carnac

Carnac is a small town on the southern coast of Brittany in France. It lies in a sheltered spot, good for farming and fishing. The area would have been an excellent place for ancient people to live, and indeed many thousands of them made it their home. We know this from the evidence they left behind, in the form of **standing stones.** Carnac is surrounded by an amazing number of ancient stones. Some are single stones called **menhirs,** but most of the stones have been laid out in a mysterious pattern.

Many of Carnac's stones are laid out in rows known as alignments.

Alignments

Spread across the landscape are lines of standing stones called **alignments.** Without actually visiting the area around Carnac, it is almost impossible to imagine the impact of these alignments when you first see them. There are thousands of stones spread across a huge area. Only later do you start to see that the stones are not just scattered randomly across the fields. Each stone has been placed deliberately in position, although the purpose is unclear.

Stone circles

Stone circles are more unusual in France than in Great Britain, but there are at least four near Carnac. Still others are slightly further away. The largest of these is Kerlescan. But one of the most interesting is at Le Ménec. The circle here is actually in the shape of an egg, but the original shape is hard to see because many stones were taken to use for building the nearby village of Le Ménec.

The circle at Le Ménec is so large that it once could have held 1,000 people. Leading toward it are eleven **aligned** avenues of standing stones, which look almost like the ropes that guide people at movie theaters or airports. The straightest of these avenues leads directly to a place where there was originally a wide gap in the circle of stones. It is not hard to imagine this straight avenue as an entranceway that could have brought hundreds of people together inside the circle.

Avebury

Just 19 miles (30 kilometers) north of Stonehenge lies another remarkable stone circle, Avebury. It is the largest stone circle in the world. The outer edge is made up of an **embankment** and ditch that are 1 mile (1.5 kilometers) long. The ditch is now partly filled, but the drop from the top to the bottom was originally 46 feet (17 meters).

Outer and inner rings

Avebury's outer ring was made up of almost 100 stones, although not all of them are still standing. Many were broken in the 1700s by builders who used the pieces of stone in their work. Several of the houses they built burned down. This only added to a feeling among local people that the stones must be **cursed.**

Inside the outer ring are the remains of two smaller stone circles. The largest stone at Avebury, the Swindon Stone, weighs about 60 tons. Like all the other stones, it was somehow moved there from another location.

This aerial photo shows the giant size of the Avebury circle. The trench was once deep enough to hide a two-story building.

Legends about Avebury

Avebury is associated with strange happenings. Each night at the stroke of midnight, the Swindon Stone is said to cross the road that runs beside it. Another stone, called the Devil's Chair, has a seat-shaped dent at its base, worn smooth by being sat on by millions of visitors. Legend says if you run around the Devil's Chair 100 times counterclockwise, the devil will appear.

The Devil's Chair at Avebury in England is surrounded by legend.

The St. Michael Alignment

Avebury is also part of a larger mystery. It is one of fifteen ancient sites that lie along an imaginary line that stretches from the far western tip of Cornwall to the eastern tip of East Anglia. This line is called the St. Michael **Alignment**. All the sites along the line are thousands of years old. No one knows how it was possible for the ancient people who built them to line them up.

The unlucky barber

During the 1300s, some of the stones at Avebury were buried on the orders of the local priest, who thought they were creations of the devil. As a worker was hollowing out a chamber underneath one of the stones, it collapsed on top of him and crushed him to death. When his skeleton was removed many years later, he was found to have a pair of scissors and a few silver coins in his pockets, making it likely that he was a barber.

More Stone Circles

Stonehenge, Carnac, and Avebury are among the most famous stone circles. But there are many more circles in England, Ireland, Scotland, France, and Africa.

The Merry Maidens and The Pipers

The Merry Maidens are a circle of nineteen stones located near the town of Penzance in Cornwall, England. Nearby stand a pair of tall stones called The Pipers. According to local legend, these are all that remain of villagers who were turned to stone for dancing on the **sabbath** day. Early Christians believed it was wrong to do anything on a Sunday except worship God.

These stones make up part of the Merry Maidens stone circle in Cornwall, England.

Drombeg

The stone circle at Drombeg in County Cork, Ireland, is known to local people as The **Druid's** Altar. For many years it was thought that stone circles had been built by the druids. Modern-day druids still worship at other stone circles, especially on **Midsummer** Day, when daylight lasts longer than on any other day of the year.

Callanish

The stone circle at Callanish is on Stornoway, one of the Outer Hebrides Islands in the Atlantic Ocean, off the west

coast of Scotland. It is a beautiful setting for a stone circle, and Callanish is surrounded by legends. One says that when the giants who lived on the island refused to become Christians, Saint Kieran turned them to stone.

Kergonan

Kergonan is one of the greatest French circles, although it is now badly overgrown with bushes and tangled weeds. It is also known as the Cercle de la Mort or as Er Anké. *Cercle de la Mort* means "the circle of death." Er Anké, a messenger of death, was a legendary figure who usually appears as a skeleton wrapped in a white **shroud.** Many stone circles are associated with death in some way. This could be because people thought the circles had been used as the sites for human **sacrifices,** or perhaps because important people were once buried there.

Wasu

Stone circles also exist in Africa, near the Gambia River. These circles seem to have been built as graveyards for important people. A small stone next to a larger one may show a child buried next to a grown-up. A V-shaped stone shows that two close relatives died on the same day and were buried next to one another.

Who Built the Stone Circles?

There have been many theories about who built the stone circles. In the Middle Ages, people said that the Romans had built them as great temples. However, the Romans were far more skillful in working with stones than the people who built the stone circles. They would have thought circles such as Avebury and Carnac were very roughly made.

Other legends said that Stonehenge was built by King Arthur or by his friend Merlin the wizard. Some even said that the stone circles were the work of the devil, who built them for his followers. For many years, people thought the stone circles had been built by **druids.** In 1974, a new theory suggested that Stonehenge had been built by Egyptian colonists. They would have found the challenge simple, having built the pyramids not long before.

Druids, shown here collecting mistletoe, were once thought to have built the stone circles.

To find the truth about who built the stone circles, scientists first had to figure out when they had been built. After World War II, a technique called **carbon dating** revealed that the circles were far older than anyone had previously realized. The oldest parts of Stonehenge, for example, date back to 3100 B.C.E. The stone-circle builders had been at work hundreds of years before the pyramids were built in Egypt. When Stonehenge was begun, the foundation stones for the Greek city of Troy had not yet been laid, the Sumerian army was just about to invent the chariot, and the ancient cultures of Central America were still 1,500 years in the future.

Scientists named the time of the stone-circle builders the **megalithic** age. *Megalith* is another word for a large stone, particularly a large **standing stone.**

Specialized equipment is used for carbon dating, which helps scientists figure out how old the circles are.

Carbon dating

*Carbon dating works by measuring the amount of a particular **element** in an object. For example, a freshly **quarried** piece of rock might have 400 pieces of the element potassium inside it. An old rock of the same type might have only 200 pieces of potassium. If scientists know that rock loses potassium at a rate of one piece every 100 years, they can figure out that the quarried rock is 2,000 years old.*

The World of the Circle Builders

What was life like for the people who built the stone circles? Could their way of life offer us any clues about what the circles were for?

One of the problems scientists face when trying to answer these questions is that the **megalithic** circle builders did not have a written language like ours. Their stories and history were remembered and retold, but never written down. So the only information we have about the megalithic world comes from things its people left behind in **burial chambers** and abandoned homes.

A wild countryside

Northwestern Europe was a very different place 5,000 years ago. There were very few fields, few cows, no sheep, and no horses. The land was almost unaffected by humans. Woodlands stretched for huge distances, and wolves could be heard howling at the moon. Travelers who journeyed into the forests needed to beware of bears. Most travelers, however, journeyed on paths made along the open ridges.

Because the circle builders left no written records, our main clues to how they lived come from objects they left behind.

Forests would have been dangerous places for the circle builders. They would have had to watch out for wolves like this one, especially at night.

The changing seasons

The circle builders lived much closer to nature than we do now. They were farmers who spent most of their time trying to grow food on poor soil with very basic tools. Bad weather in summer, when the crops should have been ripening, was a catastrophe. And long, cold winters were miserable if there was not enough food stored. The changes in seasons would have been very important to these early farmers.

The average megalithic person had a harsh, difficult lifestyle and could only expect to live for about 25 years. There are many things we have yet to discover about the world in which the people of that time lived. But the greatest mystery of all has to be this: When life was so hard, why did these people spend so much of their time building enormous stone circles?

Circles through time

*No builder who worked on one of the great stone circles would ever have expected to see his work finished. **Carbon dating** has told us that the circles took thousands of years to complete.*

Stonehenge, for example, was begun in about 3100 B.C.E., but work on the last stage of its construction was not finished until about 1100 B.C.E. Roughly 80 generations of people had been born and died in the meantime.

17

How Was Stonehenge Built?

One of the great riddles of Stonehenge is how it was built. The builders of the circle of giant **sarsen** stones had to move the stones into place and turn them upright. Then they had to lift the **lintel** stones into position on top. How they could have done this was a mystery.

Lifting the giant stones

To find out how the stones might have been lifted, scientists used computer models to test various theories. When they came up with a theory that seemed to make sense, they had to test their idea in practice. Hundreds of people using ancient tools came together to discover one of the secrets of Stonehenge. They used only the kinds of tools that would have been available to the people who built the circle.

First, the workers dug a hole. Giant levers were then used to lift one end of a stone to an angle of about 30 degrees from the ground. Then teams of helpers pulled the stone upright with ropes, so that it stood in the hole. Once two stones were in position, the lintel could be lifted into place with a wooden framework and a system of pulleys.

Bluestones from Wales

Two types of stone were used to build Stonehenge. The sarsen stones are made of hard sandstone from a site about 19 miles (30 kilometers) northeast of the circle. The smaller stones, which weigh up to four tons, are made of bluestone from the Preseli Mountains in southwest Wales. Working long before the invention of modern transportation, how

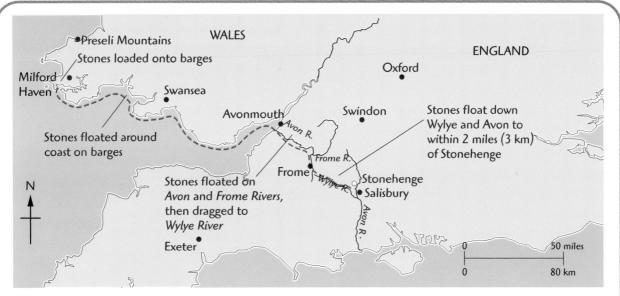

The Bluestone route

1. Stones dragged from the Preseli Mountains to Milford Haven.

2. Loaded onto barges or rafts and sailed along the coast of Wales and across to Avonmouth.

3. Floated up the Avon and Frome Rivers, then unloaded at Frome in Somerset.

4. Dragged about 6.2 miles (10 kilometers) to the Wylye River, loaded onto barges, and floated downstream to the Avon River.

5. Avon River carries stones to within about 2 miles (3 kilometers) of Stonehenge. They are unloaded and dragged the rest of the way.

could people have carried these enormous stones more than 217 miles (350 kilometers), from Wales to Salisbury Plain in England, without any machinery?

Transporting the stones required a combination of strength and cleverness. The bluestones were cut roughly into shape in the quarry. Then hundreds of men dragged them on rollers or sledges to the port of Milford Haven. They were loaded onto barges or rafts and sailed to England. Using a combination of dragging and water travel, the bluestones finally made their way to Stonehenge.

Circle Designers

After World War II, a retired professor of engineering, Alex Thom, took his tools and began to make accurate scientific measurements of stone circles. No one had ever done this before, and what Thom found seemed incredible. His discoveries caused historians to review their ideas of what the **megalithic** world had been like and led the way to solving the riddle of what purpose stone circles may have served.

Geometry of the circles

Thom found that almost all the stone circles had been built using precise mathematical knowledge. The ancient circle builders had understood **geometry** very well. They often used mathematical techniques that were not thought to have been discovered until much later. One example of this was the **Pythagorean triangle,** a triangle in which one corner is a right angle. Pythagoras, the Greek mathematician credited with inventing the formula for this type of triangle, lived from about 560 B.C.E. to 480 B.C.E. But stone-circle designers must have been using Pythagorean triangles thousands of years before this.

Pythagoras, the Greek mathematician, put into theory what stone-circle builders had put into practice.

People sometimes claim that the stones must have been put up by primitive people, because some of the "circles" are not perfect circles. Thom's survey of the circles showed that in fact the noncircular sites had been designed as either **ellipses** or elongated (stretched) circles. Both of these shapes are more complicated to design than plain circles.

The megalithic yard

Thom's most amazing discovery was that many megalithic circles had been built using a standard unit of measurement, which he called a megalithic yard. The megalithic yard had been used by hundreds of circle designers who had built circles thousands of miles apart and over a period of thousands of years. Historians had previously thought that different megalithic tribes did not share measurements. Thom's incredible findings seemed to prove this wrong.

Making a Pythagorean triangle

Circle designers worked outside on the ground, so you should too. You will need three tent stakes and a cord with thirteen knots tied in it. Tie the knots exactly the same distance apart.

1. *Put one stake through the first and last knots and into the ground.*
2. *Put another stake through the fourth knot and into the ground, keeping the cord tight between the stakes.*
3. *Now put the third stake through the eighth knot, stretch the cord tight, and push the stake into the ground.*

Congratulations! You have made a megalithic Pythagorean triangle! The measurements of the sides are 3 by 4 by 5.

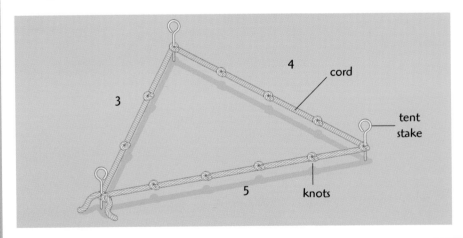

Calendars in Stone

Once scientists began to understand that the stone circles were more complicated and far more carefully designed than they had thought, they began to think about them in a different way. They also began to look more carefully at the similarities among the circles. Why did so many of them share particular features?

Midsummer and midwinter

Many circles contain stones marking the position of the sun on **Midsummer** Day or **Midwinter** Day. These dates would have been crucial to **megalithic** people. On Midwinter Day, for example, they would know that from then on the days were going to get longer. In practical terms, this meant that they would be able to figure out whether they had enough food left to last the rest of the winter. But megalithic people also would have celebrated the fact that each year was like the one before. Winter was not going to continue forever. It was going to end, just as it had the year before. The stones helped them to determine how much time was left in each season.

The sun rises behind a stone circle. As the seasons change, so do the positions of the sunrise and sunset in relation to the stones.

Predicting the seasons

Stonehenge and Avebury, for example, feature half-circles of nineteen stones. These stones are placed so that each one marks how much the sun has changed position in the sky after one year. At the end of nineteen years, the sun has returned to its original position in the sky. This does not seem particularly important to us now, but to megalithic people it would have been a different matter. Their lives depended on the seasons and the years changing in a way that they could predict. Without knowing this, they would not have been sure when to plant crops, when winter was about to arrive, or when spring would bring warmer weather.

*The sun sets at Callanish, a circle with a stone that **aligns** with the sun on Midsummer's Day.*

Computer modeling

Each year, Earth changes its position a little in relation to the sun, moon, and stars. This means that they appear in a slightly different place in the sky from one year to the next. This only makes a tiny difference, but over thousands of years it makes a noticeable difference. The stone circles were built between 3,000 and 5,000 years ago, so scientists have to use computers to figure out where the sun, moon, and stars would have appeared in the night sky at that time.

Ancient Mysteries

Using computers and modern measuring techniques, scientists have been able to provide answers to some of the questions that surround ancient stone circles. We now know how the giant stones most likely were moved to the site of the circle, how they were raised into position, and that they probably were used as a calendar. But there are other mysteries waiting to be solved. Perhaps the greatest mystery of all relates to the position of ancient sites when viewed on a map. Strange **alignments** can sometimes be seen.

Triangles on the landscape

In the west of England, the stone circle at Stonehenge and two other **megalithic** sites—Grovely Castle and the old settlement at Old Sarum—make up the three corners of a triangle with exactly equal sides, each measuring 5.6 miles (9 kilometers). If the lines that make up the sides of the triangle are continued, they each lead straight to other ancient sites.

Another, even larger triangle exists. Its three corners are Stonehenge, Lundy Island off the coast of Devon, and the site at Preseli from which Stonehenge's bluestones were **quarried.** The ancient name for Lundy is *Ynys Elen*, which means "island of the elbow" or "island of the angle."

Ley lines

Ley lines were discovered—although some people say they were invented—by a man named Alfred Watkins. In 1925, he published a book called *The Old Straight Track*, in which he claimed that the ancient sites in his local area were all connected by straight lines. He called these ley lines. The sites included stone circles, castles, **standing stones,** hilltop forts, gates, crossroads, and ancient churches—which had often been built on even older sites. Watkins's definition of a ley line was that it was a straight line on which five sites of this kind were found within 3.1 miles (5 kilometers).

Almost all stone circles are situated on ley lines. If someone can one day explain what ley lines are and how they work, it may help us to understand more about the circles. But many scientists do not accept that ley lines exist. They believe that Watkins simply found what he wanted to find. So, it could be many years before this mystery is solved.

Dowsing for ley lines

Dowsing is a mysterious art that dates back from early times. It involves using two sticks to search for underground water as a way of finding a place to dig a well. The sticks are held lightly, one in each hand. As the dowser walks over water, the sticks come together.

Some people think it is possible to dowse for ley lines. They argue that ley lines are channels of energy under the earth, which a skilled dowser can detect. There is little evidence for this theory.

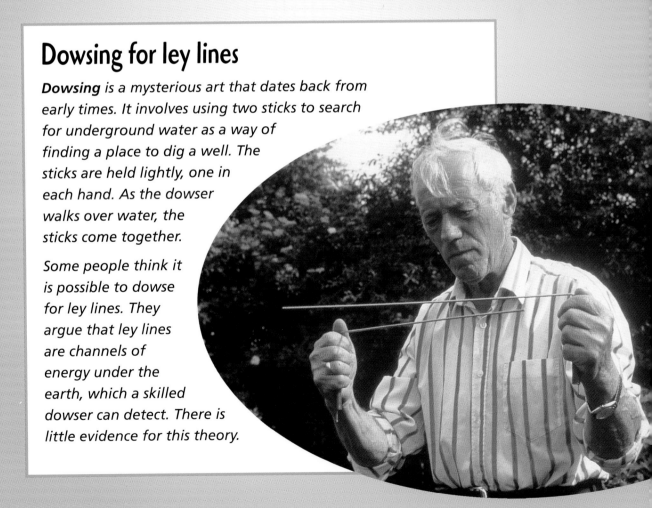

Decide for Yourself

The mysteries of the stone circles have baffled people for many thousands of years. Before modern science, people could not imagine how the circles could have been built. They gave them supernatural characteristics as a result, saying they had been made by the devil, witches, or wizards.

Today, very few people are willing to accept explanations like these. We are used to being able to understand how things work and tend to investigate until we find an explanation that is satisfactory. Then we test that explanation through experiments. This is the basis of modern science—having an idea and testing it to see if it works.

What has science shown us?

Science has offered us some insights into why the stone circles were built and for what they might have been used:

- Science has shown how **megalithic** people moved giant stones over huge distances, using a combination of dragging the stones and floating them on barges. We also know how these giant stones most likely were moved into place.
- Using **carbon dating,** scientists were able to discover the true age of stone circles. They turned out to be far older than anyone had previously guessed. Many of the stones dated from 5,000 years ago, or about 3000 B.C.E.
- Using modern surveying equipment, Alexander Thom was able to make the first proper plans of stone circles. This led Thom to suggest that the stones were laid out in a deliberate pattern and that their position meant they could be used as an enormous calendar.

- Scientists have been able to use computers to figure out what the night sky looked like when the circles were built. We now know that many circles **align** with the movements of the sun and moon.

Some mysteries remain

Some mysteries still remain unsolved. We do not yet really know what happened at the circles—were they the site of human **sacrifices** or did the bones that have been found there come from some other source? Were they used for festivals or religious ceremonies? Above all, how is it that circles and other ancient sites seem to be positioned along straight lines?

Science has not yet found a way to unravel these mysteries. But the age of the circles was a mystery until the invention of carbon dating, so perhaps in a few years scientists will be able to answer other questions about the circles. Then again, perhaps the secrets of the stone circles died out with the megalithic people, and no one will ever know the true answers.

A rainbow stretches over a stone circle in England called Long Meg and her Daughters.

Glossary

align   arrange in a straight line

alignment   group of things that are arranged in a straight line

barrow   ancient grave mound

burial chamber   room in which the body of someone who has died is kept. Burial chambers are usually either underground or partly underground.

cairn   mound of stones that is used as a monument or landmark of some kind

carbon dating   scientific method for discovering how old something is by measuring the amount of a particular element it contains

cursed   associated with evil in some way or destined to come to harm

dowsing   method of finding where water runs underground

druids   leaders of a nature-loving religion that existed in the British Isles before the time of the Roman invasion. Druidism was quickly destroyed by Christianity.

element   chemical that cannot be broken down into the different parts that make it up. Iron, gold, and potassium are all elements.

ellipse   regular oval shape

embankment   raised line of earth or stone, often used to carry a path or road or to enclose a space

geometry   branch of mathematics that is concerned with shapes and lines

gory   having to do with blood and guts

lintel   horizontal piece of wood or stone used for support

megalithic   from the time of the stone-circle builders. The name comes from the Latin words *mega*, meaning "big," and *lithos*, meaning "stone."

menhir   single standing stone

midsummer   middle of summer. Midsummer Day falls around June 21 and is the day on which it is light for the longest time.

midwinter middle of winter. Midwinter Day falls around December 21 and is the day on which it is light for the shortest time.

Pythagorean triangle triangle in which one corner is a right angle

quarried cut out of the ground. Minerals and rocks, such as coal and iron, are quarried.

sabbath weekly religious day of rest; day that is devoted to one's god

sacrifice killing an animal or person as an offering to a god

sarsen kind of sandstone that was used by stone-circle builders at Stonehenge and Avebury

shroud piece of cloth used to cover a dead body

standing stone long stone that has been stood up on end, so that it is much taller than it is wide

trilithon group of three stones, two standing upright and the third lying across the top of the gap between them

Further Reading

Oxlade, Chris. *The Mystery of Crop Circles.* Chicago: Heinemann Library, 1999.

Oxlade, Chris. *The Mystery of Life on Other Planets.* Chicago: Heinemann Library, 2002.

Oxlade, Chris. *The Mystery of the Bermuda Triangle.* Chicago: Heinemann Library, 1999.

Oxlade, Chris. *The Mystery of the Death of the Dinosaurs.* Chicago: Heinemann Library, 2002.

Index